Secrets
of the
Old Growth
Forest

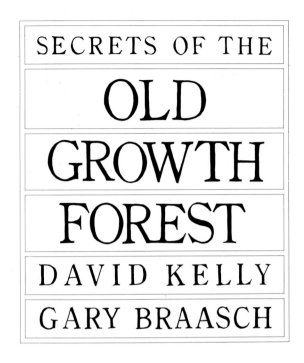

# SECRETS OF THE
# OLD
# GROWTH
# FOREST

DAVID KELLY

GARY BRAASCH

GIBBS·SMITH
P
PUBLISHER

PEREGRINE SMITH BOOKS
SALT LAKE CITY

First edition

90 89 88  3 2 1

Published by

Gibbs Smith, Publisher
P.O. Box 667
Layton, Utah 84041

Design by Smith & Clarkson

Printed and bound in Korea


**Library of Congress Cataloging-in-Publication Data**

Kelly, David, 1938–
    Secrets of the old growth forest / David Kelly; photographs by
Gary Braasch.
        p.    cm.
    ISBN 0-87905-291-0
    1. Forest conservation–Northwest, Pacific. 2. Forest ecology–
Northwest, Pacific.  I. Title
SD412.K45 1988                                                    88-5423
333.75′16′09795–dc19                                              CIP

Cover photographs by Gary Braasch:
Front cover: "Forest Floor, Oregon Cascades"
Back cover: "Indian Pipe and Oxalis"

*For Cedar, Geoffrey, Margaret and Katherine,
and other children, whose woods these are.*

# Contents

# Acknowledgments

Our first thanks must go to Gibbs Smith and Madge Baird of Peregrine Smith Books, and to Gary Soucie and Martha Hill of *Audubon* magazine, all of whom committed themselves enthusiastically to a project almost no one else understood, and who kept the faith when it looked like it was never going to be finished.

This book began when Gary Braasch read an article Jerry Franklin had written (with Richard H. Waring) for the 40th Annual Biology Colloquium held at Oregon State University in 1979. It described this forest in an entirely new way. We had seen and deplored the rapid destruction all around us; now we understood that it was an ecological disaster with worldwide implications. We called Franklin and he added our demands to an impossible workload, with unfailing generosity, off and on for eight years.

Chris Maser introduced us to the animals of the forest ecosystem and inspired us with his total commitment to education as a means of saving them. This forest has no better advocate, for he is a dynamic writer and speaker as well as a scientist.

Many other busy men and women gave freely of their energy and time. William Denison, John Carroll and John Miché introduced us to the hidden world of the forest canopy. Jim Trappe showed us how elegant a world lay just beneath the surface of the forest floor. James Sedell and his glamorous crew of shallow-water skin divers gave us a fast course in stream ecology. Kermit Cromack and Phil Sollins patiently explained something of the complex nutrient cycling that is at the heart of the forest ecosystem. John Schoen kept us posted on large mammal research in Alaska.

We also owe major debts to Chuck Meslow, Gary Miller, Art McKee, Eric Forsman, Steve Cline, Ed Starkey, Ken Cummins, Fred Swanson, Mike Wilson, Doug Smithe, Bob Tarrant, Jim Hall, Amy Ward, Gary Witmer, Cliff Dahm, Wayne McCrory, Harriet Allen and Arlene Doyle, all of whom helped educate a couple of beginners. Our apologies to those we have accidentally omitted.

Many dedicated conservationists helped us without stint. Our Canadian friends include Nick Cuff, Ken Lay and Paul George of the Western Canada Wilderness Committee, Vicky Husband of the Friends of Ecological Reserves, Victoria, and author Cameron Young of Vancouver. In the United States, Jim Monteith, Wendell Wood and Andy Kerr of the Oregon Natural Resources Council; Debbie Sease and Silvana Nova of the Sierra Club; Lynn Herring, Brock Evans, Chuck Sisco and Tom Campion, all of the Audubon Society; Jean Durning of the Wilderness Society; Susan Saul and Melvie Wong of the U.S. Fish and Wildlife Service; Rick Brown of the National Wildlife Federation; Cecelia Ostrow of the Cathedral Forest Action Group; Murray Johnson of the University of Washington; Tim McKay and his colleagues at the North Coast Environmental Center, Arcata, California; and Julie Koehler of the Southeast Alaska Conservation Council. Undoubtedly there were others, and again, we apologize.

Our final thanks go to M. J. Anderson.

*A Note on the Photographs:*

The photographs were made with Nikon equipment using lenses from 20mm to 400mm, on Kodachrome and Fujichrome. Gary Braasch gratefully acknowledges the special assistance of Doug Brazil, Dennis Wiancko, Karen and Lance Howell, Lisa McLaren, and Brian Eccles.

The authors wish to thank the following for additional (and excellent) photography: Jim Trappe and Chris Maser of Corvallis, Oregon; Tom and Pat Leeson of Vancouver, Washington; Adrian Dorst of Tofino, British Columbia; John Schoen of Juneau, Alaska; Mike Wotten of Olympia, Washington; Jeff Hughes of Anchorage, Alaska; and Ted Willcox of Vancouver, British Columbia.

*Note:* Portions of this book appeared in slightly different form in the March 1986 issue of *Audubon*.

*The outstanding scientific discovery of the twentieth century is not television, or radio, but rather the complexity of the land organism. Only those who know the most about it can appreciate how little is known about it. The last word in ignorance is the man who says about an animal or plant: "What good is it?" If the land mechanism as a whole is good, then every part is good, whether we understand it or not. If the biota, in the course of aeons, has built something we like but do not understand, then who but a fool would discard seemingly useless parts? To keep every cog and wheel is the first precaution of intelligent tinkering.*

**T**he old growth forests of the northwest coast of North America are complex associations of volcanic soil, cold rivers, hundreds of animals and plants, and a highly evolved group of conifer trees which have attained great age, size and individuality.

Its redwoods, Douglas firs, spruce, cedars and pines grow to more than 1,000 years of age, and collectively create the most massive forest on earth, exceeding even the tropical forests.

2

Each ancient tree is also a landscape unto itself in life and after its fall, supporting and in turn being influenced by thousands of specialized smaller plants, insects and animals.

Now, after 11,000 years of evolution, this great forest has nearly been exterminated by 100 years of industrial logging, just at the time when the incredible secrets of its survival are being discovered.

In the Oregon Coast Range western hemlock, Douglas fir and standing dead trees create the canopy for a rich understory of ferns, herbs and vine maple. Each large tree is a community that interacts above and in the soil to create the larger community of the forest.

SECRETS OF THE OLD GROWTH FOREST

# SECRETS OF THE OLD GROWTH

This is the forest of the Pacific Northwest. When the dense woods of the thirteen colonies were gone and the huge groves of the upper Midwest were finally logged out, this was where the axemen came next. In many ways, it was America's greatest forest, and its last.

The old growth forest curved down in a vast arc of nearly two thousand miles, from Icy Strait between Glacier Bay and Chichagof Island at the northern tip of the Alaskan panhandle, nearly to San Francisco. When Europeans first entered it in the 1700s, it had flourished undisturbed since the last ice age some eleven thousand years ago. In the northern reaches it was a mixed spruce and hemlock forest, with the giant Sitka spruce concentrated in dense pockets along the short, steep rivers and fjords. In the south were the longest-lived groves of all, the stately redwoods set back from the fierce coastal winds. Along the Oregon-California border the Siskiyou Mountains, much older than the Cascades, harbored the most complex forest of all, a mixture of many species of fir and some pockets of broad-leaf forest that were old before the first conifers took root, millions of years ago.

But the broad middle of the arc, 40 million acres spread along the British Columbian, Washington and Oregon Cascades, was dominated, behind a thin coastal strip of spruce, by the Douglas fir.

The terrain was volcanic, geologically very young, unstable. Although the great forest easily attained a biomass (weight of plants per acre) up to twice that of a mature tropical rain forest, it grew in some of the worst soils on earth: loose, steep basaltic schists poor in nearly every nutrient a plant needs, and even that was heading downhill and away, leached by the annual runoff.

(Courtesy *Sierra* magazine)

9

The weather was as bad as the soil. Rain for six months of the year, but no sun. Sun six months of the year, but scant rain. A scourge of windstorms off the Pacific most winters, and every late summer and early autumn a scourge of fire.

Yet here flourished not one, but many races of giants. A two-hundred-foot tree was ordinary. Later, when this forest had almost been destroyed, men would learn that it contained the largest living example of every major species in it. And not only the largest, but the second-largest and the third.

Here grew plants so immense that the base lived in one set of climatic conditions, the stem in another, and the crown in a third. Here were microecologies so complex that 1,500 invertebrate species might be counted on a single tree. Here was the essential home of over a hundred mammals and more resident birds than are found in any other ecosystem north of Mexico.

Here was the miracle of the old growth, one that men wouldn't notice until it was almost too late: over millions of years of adaptation; the great forest had learned to live on practically nothing.

The largest trees of the Pacific Northwest old growth, redwoods commonly attain diameters of 10 feet and heights of 300 feet in a narrow zone in northern California and southern Oregon. This is the greatest forest on earth in terms of total weight of plant life—twice as massive as the tropical forests. All but 4 percent has been logged off since the nineteenth century.

The craggy canopy of old growth in northern Washington, created as each tree reacts individually over hundreds of years to storms, wildfire, disease and the availability of light. It is home to rare and specialized lichens, voles and squirrels, and birds, as well as hundreds of other plants and animals.

# THE GROVE

A fire founded the grove. It burned for weeks across a lower slope of mountains that were not yet known as the Oregon Cascades, a few miles above the confluence of two rivers not yet called the Blue and the McKenzie. There were men and women who called them other names in fishing camps along the bank. They must have seen the smoke.

The fire burned when Christopher Columbus was still looking for a backer who would buy him a ship. When scholars in the service of Cosimo de' Medici, unpacking ancient scrolls in the brand new Library of San Marco in Florence, began studies that were the seeds of the Renaissance. The fire burned away the foliage and some of the stems of the previous forest and laid the slope open to the sun.

Seeds lying beneath the surface of the slope began to crack between the hammer and anvil of sun and frost. Seeds of the *Ceanothus*—snowbrush—that had lain here in dormant readiness for four centuries unfurled like Greek scrolls. In a year the blackened slope was a pale fresh green, while along the creek below sprang a dense thicket of young alder. Salal sprang up and in the autumns huckleberries attracted fattening bears. And after a few more

Douglas fir in the Coast Range, the most common forest giant and most economically valuable to the timber industry. The great size and clear vertical thrust of these trees also make them and their associated species among the largest and oldest living things the earth has ever created.

A species of *Brachythecium* moss stretches out along a burnt log. Large old growth trees may survive many fires due to thick bark and the forest's cool, moist atmosphere—a fact borne out in 1987 when much old forest withstood the great wildfires in the Siskiyou Mountains.

seasons darker accents appeared where Douglas fir seedlings were taking advantage of the unfiltered light.

The slope was dotted with huge standing snags and crisscrossed with massive fallen logs that the wildfire had failed to destroy because they were full of water. The logs and the roots of the snags kept the soil, gift of the previous forest, from sliding away and served as reservoirs of water and nutrients for the seedlings.

The cleared slope was invaded by rodents. Busy squirrels, voles and mice used the logs and snags for shelter as they pushed out into the burn, carrying in their intestines the spores of fungi and bacteria that could help the growth of young trees. By the time Columbus made landfall in the West Indies, the new Douglas fir grove was higher than a man's head. And for the next century it grew rapidly, a characteristic that would not be lost on men of a much later age. It was a mature forest again before

the death of Sir Walter Raleigh in 1618. "Overmature," a modern commercial forester would have thought. Overdue for the axe.

But here along this western river there were no axes. In Europe, Shakespeare harvested the ideas Florentine scholars had planted with their ancient seeds. Ships sailed, the edge of the new continent was explored and settled, a nation moved toward birth. But the grove, knowing only birdsong and the wind, endured to be utterly transformed.

Smaller fires burned parts of the grove again. There were violent windstorms some winters, and once a landslide that dammed the creek at the bottom of the slope with earth and trunks. Young, dense forest appeared again in the parts of the grove destroyed by these events, but the older trees only lost their lower branches and pushed up huge cylindrical arrays of needles on massive stems. There had always been other kinds of trees in the

In a January blizzard, western hemlocks and Douglas firs begin to catch much of the snowfall, keeping the forest floor relatively free of snow. In migrations crucial to their survival, large mammals like Roosevelt elk and blacktailed deer seek shelter and forage here when deep snow covers the meadows and clear-cuts.

The delicate blossom of a huckleberry in very early spring, symbolic of the many understory plants which are adapted to forest habitats ranging from open sun to constant shade, and which provide food at all stages of their growth for insects, animals and humans.

The needles of a
Douglas fir bejeweled
with moisture from
coastal fog. The up to
60 million needles of a
mature fir are efficient
collectors of light, more
conservative of
nutrients than
broadleaves would be,
and are so well adapted
for combing moisture
from mists that 20
percent of a forest's
annual rainfall may
actually be from needle
drip.

grove — silver fir, western red cedar, oak and yew — but now shade-loving hemlock seeded under the giants, together with a sparse understory of shrubs: salal, sword fern, Oregon grape. At every elevation, from the ground to two hundred feet, trees stretched out their surfaces to receive what the sky had to offer. There were enough needles to give this vast collection system an area of sixteen acres for each acre of forest floor. The multistoried canopy could glean light from the palest winter sun and moisture from the thinnest fog, a superb adaptation to a climate that supplied rain all through the dark winter months and withheld it entirely in the months of sunshine. The stems, living reservoirs, could hold two thousand gallons of "surplus" water against the dry summers.

Well before the signing of the Declaration of Independence the grove had changed from a simple system specializing in rapid growth into one of almost limitless complexity, a system for survival and the slow attainment of vast size. Yet it displayed an economy of means utterly beyond the designs of human technology.

Did a tree fall now and again, victim of disease? To the forest it remained a place to store water: rotten sapwood from such a log can be wrung out like a sponge. Next, bacterial action steadily concentrated the nitrogen, and chemical reaction raised the levels of phosphorus as the log decayed. Eventually the crumbling wood was entirely invaded by the rootlets of fir and hemlock, questing upward for food. In this way the log served the forest for five hundred more years, or a thousand.

Meanwhile it became den or forage ground for black bears, bobcats, lynxes, martens, skunks, salamanders, carpenter ants — at least 163 vertebrate and countless invertebrate species, each with a special role to play in the

As a fallen tree or snag decays, it becomes habitat for an increasing number of plants whose roots move into the rotting wood, breaking it apart even more. The next generation of trees, here represented by hemlock and spruce seedlings, often makes its first appearance on these "nurse logs."

19

As a tree matures the many twiggy branches that give the familiar Christmas tree shape are replaced by a relatively few giant branches, which become covered by debris, mosses and lichens. The resulting aerial landscape is home and highway to small mammals and birds adapted to arboreal living.

A red tree vole among Douglas fir needles which are its food and from which it creates its nest. This tiny creature lives its entire life in the old growth canopy—the most arboreal mammal in North America and one of the most specialized in the world. (Photo by Mike Wotten, courtesy the Burke Museum)

A very ancient forest in the Olympic Peninsula, where giant Sitka spruce are slowly being replaced by western hemlock and the forest floor consists almost completely of the rotted remains of down trees and a multitude of tiny plants.

Logging roads and clear-cuts carve deep into the forest near Prince Rupert, British Columbia. Here, as in the United States, where the Forest Service has built a road network totaling eight times the length of the Interstate Highway System, roads are commonly pushed into pristine valleys, which often prevents them from being declared wilderness.

The wrinkled bark of an ancient fir is a world of varied shelter for bats, spiders, ants and tiny mammals, and, of course, is hunting ground for woodpeckers and other predators.

forest's economy. Yet generations of forest managers were taught that this was decadence and waste.

Perhaps a branch fell from the canopy above. From its stump grew a fan-shaped array of new branches, supporting a layer of soil mulched from each season's discarded needles. Here ran the high-altitude game trails of the red tree vole, a mammal that eats needles, builds its nest of needles, even licks its moisture from needles. This nocturnal specialist lives and dies in the high canopy, although, if attacked, it can execute one of nature's most startling evasive maneuvers: a plunge of fifty feet or more straight to the forest floor, from which it nearly always scurries away unharmed.

Sharing the hidden world of the canopy with the vole, a sky garden of lichen evolved, native to the same improbable soil. It carried in the wrinkled pockets of its leaves a secret wealth: four pounds or more per acre of scarce nitrogen, captured from the atmosphere by bacterial action. A rich gift indeed to a system as conservative of nutrients as this one. It's a secret the forest would keep, with others, for five centuries.

Wars were fought and won, wagons set rolling along the Oregon Trail across Barlow Pass or down the perilous Gorge of the Columbia into an ocean of raw timber that had to be burned out of the way before a man could plant crops. To the pioneers of the 1840s and the loggers who followed, the old forest seemed limitless beyond exhaustion, profligate of its own resources, going to waste. Plumb crazy to imagine that the strategies of scarcity were what it had to teach.

So nineteenth-century man burned and logged off the broad valleys, and his farms spread out around towns with names like Amity and Sweet Home. Just before the turn of the century railways were driven through the ranges and the logs roared east. In the first years of the twentieth century the skid roads pushed up into the foothills, the small rivers were blasted clean for the spring drives, spur lines were driven up ever steeper slopes. Men went to the great wars, and those who returned wanted houses. Construction teams gouged the mountainsides for roads scarcely wider than the sixteen-gear Kenworth trucks that came down them at fifty miles an hour, brakes smoking, hellbent for the new mills in Crescent City, Eureka, Everett, Eugene, Toledo, Bellingham or Vancouver.

The giant redwoods, by far the greatest forest on earth, went the fastest, although less useful for lumber than Douglas fir. Conservationists fought big companies like Arcata and Simpson and ended up with 4 percent, most of it in roadside parks. One part of the old growth ecosystem was now virtually extinct; up north, the rush to cut the big stems speeded up.

A single ten-foot thick old growth stem was a truckload of "punkin wood," clear vertical-grain fir for fine carpentry in Chicago or Japan. And though any good carpenter will wince at the thought of it, the big logs were cheap to peel into veneer for plywood, too. A Douglas fir forest has commercial value at eight thousand board feet per acre; old growth stands can be up to ten times richer. The big companies put up new office towers in Portland and Seattle and dug into the feast. By the beginning of the 1980s, perhaps 10 percent of the old growth was left standing, almost none of it on private land.

The publicly held remainder, experts think, will last the industry for three more decades at current harvest rates. Oddly enough, that would be about the time an old growth forest would be coming into full maturity if it had been planted along with this republic in 1776.

A few miles above the confluence of the Blue and McKenzie rivers, the grove that had burned and been reborn in the age of Christopher Columbus had been requisitioned for science and escaped the saw. It was old growth now. As the boom years of Northwest logging began to wind down, the grove began to yield its secrets. At nearly five hundred years of age, it was almost exactly at the midpoint of its natural life.

**Multi-layered canopy.**

**Standing snags.**

# WHAT IS OLD GROWTH?

The old growth forests of the Pacific Northwest are ecosystems dominated by large conifers at least 250 years old and ranging beyond one thousand. Twenty-five species of conifer are found in these forests, but Sitka spruce tends to be the dominant tree in southeast Alaska and coastal British Columbia, Douglas fir in Oregon, Washington and inland B.C., and the stately coast redwood, largest of all, in northern California.

Only in old growth forest are all of the following characteristics present at the same time:

*Large living trees and a multi-layered canopy.* Old and younger trees grow together in a mixture of species. The larger trees, two hundred feet tall or more, have wind-damaged tops and relatively few large branches, with a thick growth of mosses and lichen harboring many insects, birds and small mammals. The huge trunks often survive fires, for they are reservoirs holding thousands of gallons of water protected by thick bark. The uneven canopy is efficient at trapping moisture even from thin fog during the drier seasons. Bacteria living on the leaves of certain lichen capture nitrogen, essential for plant growth, from the atmosphere.

*Large standing snags.* Standing dead snags

Down logs.

may stay erect for over two hundred years. As their branches slough off, sunlight is able to reach the forest floor, allowing species that require light, such as Douglas fir, to germinate. Insects and woodpeckers open up the dead wood, providing habitat for many other species. In turn, these become food for larger predators such as the northern spotted owl, marten and black bear.

*Large down trees.* Logs, fifty tons per acre or more in Douglas fir stands, crisscross the forest floor, helping to hold steep soils in place. As they decay over a period of two hundred to five hundred years, dozens of species of insects, birds and mammals use them for shelter or food. All this activity helps raise the concentrations of nutrients like phosphorus and nitrogen in the rotting wood, and the rootlets of nearby live trees tap them for food. Like live trees, down logs can hold extraordinary amounts of water. Often rotten sapwood from such a log can be wrung out like a sponge.

*Large fallen trees in streams.* Streams in old growth forest are shaped by it in complex ways that deserve separate treatment. See page 45.

Any one of these features may occasionally occur in younger forests; only old growth has them all.

The most celebrated
denizen of old growth,
the northern spotted
owl weighs less than
two pounds and has a
two-foot wingspan.
Owls mate for life, and
studies show that 97
percent of the nests are
in the tree-top cavities
and broken trunks that
are created only by old
growth.

# SECRETS

One deer season I knelt in a small old growth clearing, attracted by some faint scrapes in the moss, a few tufts of gray fur and two gray feathers barred with brown. An event writ small. I was a hunter, as my ancestors had been in one American woods or another since the 1640s; but here was evidence of a smaller, much more efficient hunter who had already killed today. I laid my old Mauser aside to imagine what had happened.

The flying squirrel had been already on the ground when the owl stooped. He glided down to where he or other squirrels had already identified a good place to dig, a place with food. Perhaps he dove and soared from that snag over there, old when it died, with seamed and cracked bark: good squirrel habitat. The owl was very likely watching from the lower canopy of one of these big trees, but its home was probably miles away in another of this drainage's isolated patches of old growth, or in another drainage altogether. The movement of the squirrel caught the owl's night vision. There would have been no hesitation, no moment of doubt such as human hunters always endure: range, windage, lead of the moving target, chance of missing and wounding, ethics, greed, reluctance, decision.

Northern flying squirrel, an arboreal creature who can glide up to 150 feet through the forest to reach its favorite meals of succulent lichens, fungi and truffles. The squirrel is one of 45 vertebrate animals that require the cavities of old growth trees, snags and down logs. (Photo by J. W. Grace, USFS, courtesy Chris Maser)

Instead the owl saw and stooped. A creature who must eat its weight in quarry every day takes all chances. No doubt the squirrel leapt under similar compulsion. What had it been after?

The northern spotted owl is the only species whose survival has been proven to depend on old growth. For at least a dozen other species, ranging from the marten to the pileated woodpecker, a reservoir of old growth habitat may also be essential. But using radio collars, Oregon State University researcher Eric Forsman followed foraging flights from owl nests in the broken tops of ancient Douglas firs and fed the data into a computer. The computer generated maps that show an overwhelming preference for hunting in forest that is over two hundred years old, even if to do so the owls have to travel to the limits of their ranges, bypassing plenty of slightly younger forest en route to a kill. The owl needs old growth, and lots of it. But he probably won't get it.

Early in the 1980s government biologists decided that of the 1,000 or so nesting pairs of northern spotted owls in Oregon, for example, 400 were needed to guarantee survival of the species. They initially proposed setting aside 1,000 acres for each nesting pair. Later studies showed an average pair needed 2,200 acres and in some conditions of terrain, well over 3,000. But Bureau of Land Management timber managers agreed to a mere 300 acres per pair when, as part of an interagency agreement, it took responsibility for 90 owls. Later the agency's director circulated a staff memo pointing out that this was an informal agreement and that the Bureau had no legal obligation to honor it if it interfered with timber sales.

Forsman reported his findings in 1976. In the summer of 1985 University of Chicago population geneticist Russell Lande completed a computer analysis of all available information about the owl and its habitat. It concluded that under prevailing management plans the owl was headed for certain extinction. But in 1987 USFS and U.S. Fish and Wildlife officials consulted each other and decided not to list the owl as threatened or endangered.

Considered by itself, the owl does not pose much of an obstacle to those who wish to go on cutting the old growth. Indeed, it is politically expedient to focus attention on a single species whose insignificant existence stands in the way of thousands of jobs and billions of dollars in public and private revenue.

Inconveniently for the industry, the little owl has turned out to be anything but insignificant. Beginning in 1968, a few scientists began to apply the new techniques of ecosystems research to this forest. Ecosystems research is politically awkward; it considers nothing by itself. In the Douglas fir forests of the Cascades and the Coast Ranges the owl's ecological role is to cull and keep healthy the population of small mammals that are its favorite foods, among them the fungus-eating California red-backed vole and the northern flying squirrel.

A flying squirrel would not launch himself into space from the safety of an old-growth fir's wrinkled bark, nor a vole emerge from his burrows under an old-growth down log, were they not also gourmets. They are after truffles.

The significance of these risk-takers, their roles in the forest's total ecology, was explained in 1977 by two scientists from different disciplines working as a team, as ecosystems researchers often do. Chris Maser was then a biologist working for the BLM and writing a voluminous resource book on forest mammals. Jim Trappe was a mycologist, a mushroom expert attached to the Forest Service.

It has been known for a century that woody plants, and especially conifers, develop symbiotic relationships between the tips of their roots and certain fungi. These fungus-root combinations are called mycorrhizae. But their full interconnectedness with the forest ecosystem was not widely understood, even among botanists, until Maser and Trappe published a short article with the whimsical title "Ectomycorrhizal Fungi: Interactions of Mushrooms and Truffles with Beasts and Trees."

Maser and Trappe explained that when the fungi wrap themselves tightly about the root tips, even penetrating the outer cellular layers,

**Mammalogist Chris Maser, spokesperson for old growth.**

they perform the spongelike services fungi do best: absorbing minerals, nitrogen and water from the soil and feeding them to the tree. They also produce growth-regulating chemicals that induce the tree to produce new root tips and that strengthen the tree's immune system, giving it a longer life span. In trade for all this, the tree supplies sugars that the chlorophyll-lacking fungi can't manufacture for themselves.

Squirrels, mice and voles, along with certain insects, eat the fruiting bodies of the fungi—truffles—and carry the spores to new sites in their intestines. Though some mycorrhizal fungi fruit above ground as mushrooms and scatter their spores on the wind, truffles are entirely earthbound. Unless animals eat them, they don't reproduce. And it is these fungi that are adept at conserving moisture on the steep slopes where ground water runs off rapidly and where foresters have a hard time

growing new trees.

As their spores ripen the truffles begin to emit strong and distinctive odors—fruity, fishy, cheesy, garlicky—so that the rodents can home in on them with a minimum of digging. Squirrels that, for whatever reason, can't do this efficiently enough, of course, get eaten by owls.

Some animals habitually deposit the spores nearby, where they aid existing trees. Others, edge-dwellers like Townsend's chipmunks, deer mice, Mazama pocket gophers and heather voles, seem to specialize in moving the spores out into clear-cuts, burns, meadows and, in the case of Mt. St. Helens, volcanic mudflows, where they are ready to aid pioneering seedlings. All these rodents also ingest and carry nitrogen-fixing bacteria to the same sites.

"Keep in mind," wrote Maser and Trappe, "that these functions have evolved by natural

At the end of summer, this five-month-old spotted owl has left the nest even though its plumage is still developing. Due to lack of habitat and predation from larger species of owls who do not need old growth, the survival rate for baby spotteds is less than 10 percent, which could mean extinction of the species.

**James Trappe, mycologist, in search of truffles in a decomposing log.**

selection over millions of years."

Maser and Trappe were members of an informal group of scientists studying the old growth under the informal leadership of Dr. Jerry Franklin, then chief plant ecologist of the Forest Service's Pacific Northwest Forest and Range Experiment Station, based in Corvallis, Oregon. Franklin was the most distinguished man in his field and had been an officer of the National Science Foundation. He knew how to make money flow to projects he considered worthwhile. Roughly between 1970 and 1985 Franklin and his associates conducted what amounted to a Manhattan Project of the north woods, informally of course. Not until the 1981 publication of their preliminary findings in a forty-eight page technical report entitled *Ecological Characteristics of Old Growth Douglas Fir Forests,* did they start to become *personae non grata* in certain circles.

Franklin and his seven coauthors, who included Maser, described a system a great deal more complex and subtle than the models generated by earlier forest science. In the hundreds of individual studies that lay behind the little booklet no theme was more common than the unexpected finding, the surprising result. The forest worked in ways we hadn't dreamed.

To the scientific audience, this was good news. "We are hard up worldwide for systems that work," enthused William Denison, a botanist who led trained mountain climbers in pioneering explorations of the forest canopy. "This whole ecosystem is an intellectual resource. It gives you access to stuff you can't imagine."

But reactions to these findings in government and industry have varied according to how various slices of bread were buttered. Weyerhaeuser Corporation, a company with vast tree farms, hired Trappe as a consultant

A tiny landscape with immense ramifications is this section of decomposing log being invaded by roots of young hemlock in search of the moist, nutrient-laden layers within. The mushroom is a *Russula emetica*, which, like those that fruit underground, creates mycorrhizal associations with tree roots.

and set about inoculating the roots of its young trees with mycorrhizal fungi, using its employees in the role of mice. Willamette Industries, a company heavily dependent on federal timber sales, continued to heap scorn on what its chief executive officer, William Swindells, Jr., called the Billion-Dollar Owl. The Reagan Administration in its first term announced large funding increases to support timber production at a time when the recession had virtually shut down the timber industry, and shrugged off suggestions that it had concocted a scheme to auction off the future of the national forests while prices were low. It quietly terminated four hundred research positions and dried up the funding for several old growth projects, including a five-year study of the habitat requirements of old growth animals it had itself proposed, a sugar coating for the planned increases in harvest.

By the mid-1980s ecosystems research was distinctly out of fashion with young government scientists hoping to further their careers. But in 1984 Maser and Trappe published another USFS general technical report entitled *The Seen and Unseen World of the Fallen Tree*. It directly contradicted a hypothesis that both the industry and the Forest Service have always held, and have exported all over the world *via* teams of traveling consultants. Just incidentally, it's a hypothesis that seems to dictate the speedy elimination of old growth for big profits.

Large logs on land are a main structural component of the old growth and the one most often cited as evidence that these are decadent forests, going to waste. Or, as industry consultant Robert Vincent put it to a conference, that "they are ecosystems built on functions of death; complex, different, and unusual ecosystems that contribute little to others and are extremely self-centered in that they care

**Marbled murrelet. (Alaska Department of Fish and Game, Jeff Hughes)**

**Pileated woodpecker. (Photo copyright Ted Willcox)**

# CITIZENS OF THE OLD GROWTH

At least 118 vertebrate species have their primary habitat in old growth; of these, 41 can find their nesting, breeding or forage grounds nowhere else. Often this is because they require some feature or features, such as large standing snags or a high density of large down timber, that only old growth forest can produce. Availability of prey species is also crucial: two-thirds of the vertebrate species found in old growth are predators.

The list of species that depend entirely or largely on old growth is continually growing. An animal like the spotted owl, who can nest only in the broken tops of old growth firs and who forages only in old growth, is doubly doomed as the forest vanishes. But recently researchers have noticed that populations of the secretive marbled murrelet, a robin-sized seabird that can literally fly underwater in pursuit of small fish, have been declining on almost the same curve as the owls. Although the murrelet nests on the open tundra along parts of the Alaskan coast, it apparently nests only in virgin forest from southeast Alaska down to the southernmost extent of its range in central California. When coastal old growth is cut, the seagoing murrelet disappears.

This information is so recent that the murrelet is not on any threatened or endangered species lists—though it is listed as a "species of special concern" in parts of California, where only 4 percent of the coast redwood forest survives. How many more species may be in trouble without our knowing it?

Sometimes the relationship between a species and the old growth habitat is perfectly obvious. In the cold wet winters of southeast Alaska, the Sitka blacktailed deer *always* needs the protection and available forage of high density, low elevation old growth. But sometimes it is not obvious. The Roosevelt elk of the Oregon and Washington coast ranges, heavier-bodied cousin of the more familiar Wapiti of the Rocky Mountains, may range happily outside old growth boundaries until that once-in-a-decade, extremely severe winter comes along. Then, if there is no old growth shelter available, the Roosevelt herds can be decimated.

Here are listed some of the species whose dependence on old growth is the most obvious. They will surely decline sharply if the cutting continues. But so will many more that we cannot yet predict. Aldo Leopold's injunction to "keep every cog and wheel" never seemed more urgent than in old growth.

*northern goshawk*
*bald eagle*
*osprey*
*northern spotted owl*
*Vaux's swift*
*pileated woodpecker*
*Hammond's flycatcher*
*Townsend's warbler*
*red crossbill*
*marbled murrelet*
*long-eared myotis bat*
*silver-haired bat*
*northern flying squirrel*
*long-legged myotis bat*
*bushy-tailed wood rat*
*red tree vole*
*California red-backed vole*
*white-footed vole*
*marten*
*fisher*
*Sitka blacktailed deer*
*Roosevelt elk*
*Pacific giant salamander*
*Siskiyou salamander*
*Olympic salamander*
*Oregon salamander*
*clouded salamander*
*tailed frog*

Due to estuary and forest destruction in southeast Alaska the mountain goat, river otter and giant coastal grizzly bear are seriously threatened there, and probably in British Columbia as well.

**Pine marten. (Photo copyright Tom and Pat Leeson)**

**Sitka blacktailed deer. (Photo copyright John Schoen)**

**Pacific giant salamander.**

Old growth ecologist
Jerry Franklin, in his
research forest near the
Blue River in Oregon.

The bark has sloughed off this well-decomposed log, revealing the Gothic maze of ant and termite galleries in which prowl predatory insects and tiny vertebrate animals, and through which tree roots search upwards for the water that a log can retain even in the driest of summers.

only for themselves and no one else. . . . They fill a limited function, as does a cemetery."

A flabbergasted Jerry Franklin, who was present at the same conference, commented, "I'll bow to Bob Vincent on that. Life does run on death." But neither he nor anyone else knew how to react to the bizarre anthropomorphic notion that the old growth was not worth saving because it didn't care!

In *The Seen and Unseen World* Maser and Trappe take us on a guided tour through the maze of plant and animal interactions that occur inside a log as it decays, and "decay" itself is seen as the sum total of that lively burrowing, scurrying, rooting and growing activity. The seen world of the forest permutates a simple set of nutrients into ever more complex adaptations, increasing the chances that the whole system will survive. The unseen world of the fallen tree *uses* a complex series of adap-

tations to break wood down, releasing in the process a simple set of nutrients. Decay is merely a counterpoint, life and death a single process, like a mirror fugue conceived by a composer even better than Bach.

The decay process starts as an intricate cooperation between bacteria, boring insects and fungi. At first, the tree lacks interior surfaces that can be attacked. Microorganisms smaller than the spaces between the wood fibers themselves are the first entrants and begin the decay process by softening the sapwood. A bark beetle chews through the bark and connects the outside world to the tree. His waste introduces fungal spores and more bacteria. Soon he is joined by other wood eating insects: mites, termites, carpenter ants and many other species each preparing habitat for some other to follow, each adapted to process a different part of the tree. Predators ranging from small spiders to sizable salamanders

This tiny Oregon salamander is among a specialized group of reptiles that stalks the termite galleries of down logs in search of springtails, mites, spiders, beetles and ants.

40

and newts hunt the ant galleries, and a food chain ultimately leading to animals as large as shrews and moles develops. The cambrium and sapwood is easy to get at and easy to digest—fast food. As the levels of "free" nutrients in the log drop, consumers with more complex and capable digestive systems replace simpler feeders. They attack the dense heartwood and the process of ingestion and structural change continues, a part of what California

The California red-backed vole, the "citizen par excellence" of the forest, is a gourmet whose tastes run almost exclusively to mushrooms. Its coevolution with the great trees and the underground truffles, whose roots aid in their growth, is a unique relationship that occurs only in this forest.

Shelf fungi are usually indicative of disease deep within a living tree, but the weakness that results serves the forest as a creator of snags—standing dead trees that become crucial habitat and hunting ground for bats, birds and mammals. This particular fungus is *Phaeolus schweinitzii*, growing on a hemlock.

41

Unexpected jewel in the forest setting, the golden buprestid beetle is one of a family of insects whose adults eat tree needles and lay eggs in the bark of newly fallen trees. When the larvae hatch, they bore into sapwood or even heartwood, starting the invasion of decomposers. (USDA Forest Service, C. Maser and J. Trappe)

nature writer John Daniel so beautifully terms the forest's "slow looping dance through time."

As the log slumps to the ground—a process that may take decades on some sites—tunneling animals like the California red-backed vole begin to use it for shelter and, since in advanced stages of decay the log is a host for many truffles, forage. This tiny (less than two hundred millimeters long, an ounce or less in weight), mouselike creature digs its burrows beneath the logs and completes the same symbiosis with fungi and tree roots as does the flying squirrel. But unlike the squirrel, who eats more arboreal lichen than anything else, the red-backed vole subsists almost entirely on truffles—the only vertebrate that does. He is the citizen par excellence of the forest floor: his whole existence depends on the death of some trees and makes possible the life of others. And, of course, he is also part of a food chain, prey to martens, weasels, spotted

skunks and bobcats, as well as owls. When a low population of redbacks is indicated by the absence of predators, the forest is in deep trouble.

Maser and Trappe list a "grossly simplified" series of animal-plant-nutrient minisystems that occur, one after the other, within the log over hundreds of years. First come animals that eat the fallen tree and open it to the outside world so that nutrients can begin to move around: wood-boring beetles, carpenter ants, termites and wood-tunneling mites. They open pathways for microorganisms that grow on the fallen tree: bacteria, yeasts and ambrosia fungi. Next come animals that eat such microorganisms: springtails, mites, and ambrosia beetles. Live plants, such as western hemlock and huckleberry, that form specific symbiotic relationships with fungi come next; both the plants and the fungi root in the wood as it is opened up and begins to fragment. Animals that eat

A centipede curls protectively around its mass of eggs as it is unexpectedly exposed to daylight by a forest researcher. The total number of invertebrate animals that inhabit even a single large decomposing log is still unfathomable to scientists, and an unknown number of species remain to be discovered.

An adult spotted owl, hunting at every opportunity night and day to feed its young, brakes as it judges the movement of its prey. By tracking mated pairs of owls with radio collars, ornithologists have calculated home ranges of more than 3,000 acres per pair. The U.S. Forest Service plans to set aside about 2,000 acres each for a limited number of pairs.

animals—predators—enter the log's system whenever they find a food supply and the right access: mites, spiders, pseudoscorpions, centipedes and salamanders roam and hunt in galleries prepared by other insects. Last come animals that eat dead plant and animal material and animal feces: earthworms, mites, millipedes, isopods, earwigs.

All of these teeming populations become food for vertebrate predators—birds, small mammals, even bears.

All these activities release nutrients that have been stored within the tree during its life or that have accumulated from leaf litter or other downfall, as well as from rainwater that picks up nutrients on its way through the canopy—for a fallen tree can still accumulate as well as spend chemical wealth.

Every bit of the log is made available to living, growing plants, especially trees, and in forms they can readily use. Absolutely noth-

ing is wasted. If this constitutes uncaring selfishness, the mind boggles at what generosity would be like.

One of the most striking points in *The Seen and Unseen World* is the sheer size of the phenomenon being studied: from 50 to 265 tons of down wood *per acre* in an old growth forest; the even higher numbers in streams reflect the fact that waterlogged wood excludes oxygen and thus decays more slowly. The evidence suggests that there is as least as much nutrition lying on top of the forest soil as in it.

Yet until quite recently everyone concerned supposed that these were the signs of decadence and death. Good forest management meant cleaning up the mess. Clear-cuts were burned to eliminate the debris and streams were "de-snagged" with the aim of improving water quality! The effects of this will be discussed later; but the immediate effect on

A stream in old growth with gravel bars, gentle waterfalls, and back waters created by abundant woody material.

# SECRET LIFE OF A STREAM

Fallen trees lie in random patterns in small head-water streams. Since the run-off is not powerful enough to dislodge them, such logs form semi-permanent "stairsteps" that hold woody debris long enough for 70 percent of it to be processed by insects and bacteria.

Midges are among the early colonists in such logs. They tunnel into the outer layers and create entry for algae and microbes which, in turn, feed grazing insects. Shredders, such as caddis flies and stone flies, familiar to trout fishermen, ingest wood that has been softened by fungi. Scrapers, such as the mayfly, and raspers, such as snails, eat not only the soft wood but also the assemblage of minute organisms, called the periphyton, that grow on its surface. Over decades of colonization by fungi, oxygen slowly invades the softened wood; finally earthworms penetrate.

Many more insects use the roughened wood for shelter than consume it, including boring semi-aquatic beetles and fly larvae. The galleries they open up are used again and again by insects that do not bore, such as the crane fly. Net-spinning caddis flies, who filter food from the water, find such textured wood surfaces ideal for attaching their nets.

Fish not only consume these insects and their predators, but rely on the pool-forming ability of the forest for shelter from storm run-off and for temperature control. Studies show that populations of large salmonids, such as coho salmon and cutthroat trout, are directly related to pool volume on a stream. Given a choice between pools, large fish always congregate in the one with the most large woody debris.

Even when streams become small rivers, too wide for logs to bridge, snags lying in the water and across the secondary channels and sloughs on flood plains provide important habitat.

Fish are an end product of the old growth forest. In *The Seen and Unseen World of the Fallen Tree,* James Trappe and Chris Maser point out that "carbon, nitrogen, and all the other materials that leave a watershed either pass through or accumulate in the stream environment, which encompasses less than one percent of the watershed area. Such a concentration of nutrients, the capacity of a stream to store organic material, and the efficiency to process it depend on the number and quality of fallen trees in the stream."

When Northwest fisheries declined disastrously after World War I, overfishing was blamed. Recent research, notably by Oregon State University biologist James Sedell, suggests that this was, instead, the consequence of the destruction of old growth in the Coast Ranges, an ecosystem distress signal that no one understood.

An ancient western red cedar grips a hillside in the Cascades against a backdrop of down logs. The weight of fallen trees—averaging 53 tons per acre—exceeds that of living trees, but the two parts are really one: a tree that stood for 800 years may serve the forest another 500 years after its fall.

forest managers of the findings of Franklin, Maser and their associates is typified by the reaction of one grizzled old-timer, called into a meeting to get the latest word:

"First you guys told us to clean up the streams. Then you told us to leave the mess in the streams. First you told us to burn slash. Now you say we need slash. And now . . .," he struggled for words, "now you're telling me that I have to manage for *mouse shit*."

By 1987 Chris Maser felt it necessary to leave the Bureau of Land Management. One of his senior colleagues explained, "I have to hand it to [the BLM's forest managers]. They used to practice rape and call it consent. Now they're practicing rape and calling it rape."

The findings were being largely ignored. The slash burning and the clear-cutting of prime old growth went on.

Jerry Franklin, a Camas, Washington, mill-worker's son who had refused several prestigious academic offers to stay in the Forest Service, now accepted a professorship at the University of Washington. He retains a half-time connection with the agency he served so loyally. The pioneering epoch of research into the old growth was winding down after nearly two decades of work.

Franklin spent much of his last few years at the Pacific Northwest Forest and Range Experiment Station as a traveling salesman for old growth. That meant putting in as much time aboard airplanes as in the lab or in the H. J. Andrews Experimental Forest. There the grove we saw grow to 500 years of age has been divided into "reference stands" and equipped with rain gauges, leaf-collector screens, and instruments to measure heat and moisture.

The forest is still Franklin's natural habitat, however rarely he might be sighted in it. Here he is relaxed and happy as he hops over down logs and simultaneously discusses experiments with Art McKee, director of the scientific program on the Andrews.

"Now what I would like to do is to cut about a hundred of those twenty-one-inch stems and do a *real* log decomposition study," he announces. Sections of the trunks would be hauled to carefully selected sites and every decade or so researchers would saw a slice from each sample for laboratory analysis.

McKee is nodding. They are actually planning to do this. But how long is such a study going to take? "About 250 years."

The view from a light plane almost anywhere over the Northwest puts such a plan in a strikingly ironic perspective. Neither the timber industry nor the Forest Service is waiting to do a 250-year decomposition study. A typical drainage resembles an insect-chewed leaf rather than the reassuring Forever Green of the official maps. Into this devastation the young of the nesting spotted owls fly out to make their way. Most of them don't survive. The thinly scattered predators of the Cascades and the Coast Ranges are wandering through the shreds of their habitats like refugees in a war zone. William Denison and some other scientists think the ecosystem may already have shrunk to a point where maladaptation, or "genetic drift," is starting to occur. Five years before conservationists began talking about a moratorium on logging trees over two hundred years old, he was advocating it. "Suppose we wished to conserve the Jewish gene pool for its characteristics of creativity and productivity," he asked. "Would it be enough to set aside Manhattan?"

Saying goodbye at the intersection of two remote logging roads high in the Cascades, Jerry Franklin put it as baldly as a man still earning a living as a career forester could. "How much of the genetic base are we willing to lose? How much profit are we going to be able to deny ourselves for future generations? These are social and moral issues, not scientific ones. But you don't close out options when you don't have to. You don't have a right to, in effect, mine the productivity of the earth. And you don't have a right to eliminate species."

Franklin ducked into a Dodge compact from the government car pool. He was a couple of hours of dirt road from another airplane to another timber industry conference, this time in Anchorage. He grinned.

"They aren't going to like what I have to say."

47

It was one log to a railroad car in 1908 in the North Cascades. (Photo by Darius Kinsey, courtesy Oregon Historical Society)

# THE GREEN HELL

The forest was the Heart of American Darkness. Nathaniel Hawthorne, close to the hearthfire in his snug Berkshire retreat, caught a sense of it as he struggled to outdo his friend Herman Melville horror for horror. To the nineteenth-century American mind it was still an unfathomable physical and moral chaos in which a Young Goodman Brown might lose himself—or his soul—by a single misstep. It surrounded us. There was a savage or the Devil behind every tree. Our role models, like Daniel Boone, were those who could stand the forest's isolation, who could navigate it unscathed and carve on its trunks that they had "kilt a bar." Clearing the land of it was the first great national occupation—to plant corn, yes, but also to create fields of fire. A man is happiest with a clear shot. We are a race of edge-dwellers.

Men who converted the forest to personal wealth didn't forfeit our admiration. Paul Bunyan and his Blue Ox were created to be corporate symbols. They were bigger than the trees they cut, a celebration and sanctioning of megalomania, but we took them for folk heroes.

The real loggers of the pre-chainsaw era, tougher even than the real cowboys, were ignorant of all but their work and customarily

Standing on springboards to get above the swelling butt, two turn-of-the-century loggers are ready to hand-fall this Sitka spruce. Their term for the long bucksaw waiting on the right was "misery whip." (Oregon Historical Society)

"The Green Hell" in southern Oregon, about 1914. Trestles converge across devastated forest toward a rough camp of the Coos Bay Lumber Company. (Oregon Historical Society)

broken by it. To them the forest was "the Green Hell." A logger was "Pops" or "Dad" if he lived to be thirty.

A tree he was topping could scissor and tear him in half as he hung from climbing spurs and belt. An entire two-hundred-foot stem might split lengthwise and crush the loggers who were "falling" it, or it might explode like a bomb when it hit the ground, filling the air with shrapnel. In the mills, the huge steam driven bandsaw blades often ran night and day until they broke, killing whomever happened to be in the way. In one Gray's Harbor, Washington, mill such a blade killed two men and fetched up coiled in a corner, its kinetic energy still intact. No one dared touch it, so masons were summoned to brick it in. Then work resumed.

Twice a day, loggers in the camps had fifteen minutes in the cookhouse to eat, in total silence, the invariable beans, bacon and flapjacks. The rest of the time off shift they slept. Perhaps three times a year they went to town to be stripped of their wages in such establishments as Portland's legendary Erickson's, a bar that ran around all four sides of a city block. Erickson's had a theater, dance hall, casino and restaurant in the middle and whores in the cribs upstairs. The place got a new floor every year, the old one having been worn down to the joists by caulk boots.

In any logging town the men could be plucked clean, given a dose of the clap, and be back in the hiring hall in less than a week, unless they were shanghaied—a distinct possibility. In many of the bars and sporting houses in Portland and Seattle trap doors opened above tunnels that led straight to the docks.

Logging today is still dangerous, though the safety standards are higher. But the greatest threats to a logger's paycheck are not accidents or the risk of being shanghaied at Erickson's.

51

And still they fall: logging on the Willamette National Forest, Oregon, in the 1980s. In a logging euphemism this is called "harvesting overmature timber," a phrase which begs the question of whether we can harvest what we didn't plant and don't plan to let grow back.

The industry employee of the 1980s faces the high probability of being replaced by an automated mill and the absolute certainty that, in his lifetime or his son's, overcutting will permanently eliminate the job. Overcutting—the removal of timber faster than it can grow back—is going on at a rate as high as 70 percent on some Northwest national forests, and a cut 40 percent over replacement is routine. It's a situation that would have seemed unimaginable to the "timber beasts" of the early 1900s.

Around the turn of the century the Northwest metropolises were seized by longings for gentility. Veneration of nature was the fashion of the day and Burroughs and Muir were its prophets. Timber barons in Portland helped create a scenic highway and a chain of parks in the Columbia Gorge, but the forests further from town still seemed limitless beyond any need to conserve.

Teddy Roosevelt, however, recognized that the forests were finite in the West just as they had proved in the upper Midwest. Gifford Pinchot, the man Roosevelt chose to bring the Forest Service into being, believed in "even-flow" management of the federal lands. Each national forest could take out in a year only as much as it grew in a year. You harvested the interest, never the capital. And for nearly half a century the agency embodied Pinchot's ideal.

In the years just after World War II, however, there was great political pressure to do more to alleviate the housing crunch, and the Forest Service began to respond with some redefinitions. It was suddenly acceptable to cut more than the forest could produce now if the land could be reasonably expected to grow the timber back at some later date, when funds for reforestation were appropriated. Percentages of the land to be harvested were meas-

52

ured not just against the total of commercial timber in the forest but against that plus land that would never grow a tree. "Allowable cut" no longer meant a limit never to be exceeded but a quota to be met. As professional foresters looked forward to comfortable positions in the industry after retirement, the mandate for multiple-use was ignored and lands allocated for habitat or recreation tended to be high up in the mountains, covered with rock or ice.

The annual struggle to get a share of the budget and the natural bureaucratic tendency to accrete power and protect jobs encouraged another change: road building became the largest enterprise within the agency.

Even the idea that the national forests should produce, rather than consume, revenues was forgotten, except in rhetoric at appropriation time. Most timber sales were subsidized by the public. The Wilderness Society recently estimated that over the next ten years, for example, American taxpayers will have to dig into their pockets to cover a loss on timber sales of *two billion dollars*. That's the result of management such as we saw on the Tongass National Forest in the mid-1980s when the Service lost roughly ninety cents on every dollar it spent marketing its timber.

The Tongass is a paradigm of waste. Although it is America's largest national forest on the map, less than 5 percent of its rugged terrain is in high-volume timber. By a mandate of Congress and as a trade-off for lands taken out of timber production by the Alaska Wilderness Bill, this small percentage can be cut at a much faster rate than any forest could possibly sustain. Most of the productive land is found at low elevations along coves and small rivers, and constitutes the essential habitat of most of America's bald eagles, the largest concentration of grizzly bears left on earth, and 40 thousand Sitka blacktailed deer who are utterly dependent on old growth cover. These groves also protect the spawning grounds of a commercial salmon fishery that, while still relatively undeveloped, grosses nearly $100 million a year, costs the government almost nothing, and generates far more jobs than the whole southeast Alaskan timber industry.

Most of the marketable timber is concentrated along the glorious Inside Passage, which generates some 3,200 jobs for southeast Alaska annually (as opposed to approximately 1,400 in timber operations). The tourists are not paying to see clear-cuts.

The Lisianski River drainage on Chicagof Island is exemplary of what is happening to southeast Alaska's small watersheds. The Lisianski is one of the finest wild salmon streams left in North America. Writing in *Audubon*, George Laycock reported its worth at $400 thousand in salmon annually. The drainage abounds in bear, deer and geese as well. The old-growth timber along the river corridor is slated to be logged. It should bring the government some $40 thousand.

Many tidal estuaries such as this one are scheduled for cutting in northern British Columbia and southeastern Alaska during the next few years. The result will be stunning losses not only of the forest ecosystem but also of the rich fish and marine life that will be choked out by logging slash, silt and increased water temperature.

Black bear and salmon play out the complex relationship among large predators, anadromous fish and the old growth forest. Forest destruction, much more than overfishing, is a major reason for the sharp decline in Northwest fisheries in this century. (Photo copyright Tom and Pat Leeson)

Southeast Alaska and
coastal British
Columbia, where this
pair defends its nest
and young, are home to
the greatest
concentration of bald
eagles in the world,
who rely on many types
of old growth trees for
nest sites.

This seemingly endless clear-cut across miles of southern Vancouver Island is evidence of the vengeance with which logging has been undertaken in British Columbia. Employing about 20,000 fewer workers now than in the early 1980s, the B.C. timber industry still cuts 300,000 acres of old growth each year.

The costs of getting that timber out, however, involve an estimated $1.6 million for roads and other costs which will bring the total close to $3 million. The Lisianski, a landscape of heartbreaking beauty and known productivity, is being sacrificed to what amounts to a federal welfare project, surely the least efficient in our history. And it is not alone.

Using accounting procedures accepted by the Forest Service, the General Accounting Office estimated a loss of $22 million on the Tongass in 1986 alone. The Sitka spruce had few buyers.

The principle beneficiaries of this policy have been two companies, Alaska Pulp Co., owned by Japanese, and Louisiana Pacific/Ketchikan. The latter company had been under Justice Department investigation in a price fixing scandal when Ronald Reagan appointed its parent corporation's general counsel, John Crowell, to be Assistant Secretary of Agriculture in charge of the Forest Service. One of the hunting guides in Juneau, watching his livelihood vanish along with the brown bear habitat, commented, "I assume he washed his hands first."

In a quid pro quo for his support of the 1980 Alaska National Interest Lands Conservation Act, Senator Ted Stevens insisted on an addition to the bill that mandated 450 million board feet of timber annually to the two companies, and requiring the treasury to provide $40 million annually for the purpose, ". . . or as much as the Secretary of Agriculture finds is necessary." This not only assured the destruction of the Tongass, which no one imagined could support such a cut, but signed a blank check for the Forest Service. In the more than seventeen years since, the Tongass has become famous for its "roads to nowhere," and for such items as a headquarters complex, complete with recreation facilities and cable TV, that sits unoccupied in the outback.

Both Alaska Pulp and Louisiana Pacific have unprecedented fifty-year contracts with the Forest Service. But the timber will be long gone before they expire.

Things are even worse in British Columbia, which boasts the world's largest clear-cut (twenty-five miles long and up to twenty-four miles wide, it could be seen from an orbiting space shuttle without a telescope). Virtually all the remaining old growth in the province is scheduled for quick harvest under a curious institution called a Tree Farm License, which has nothing to do with tree farming. Under this

Alaska cedar left behind in a Queen Charlotte Islands clear-cut. In British Columbia, as much as 25 percent of the valuable timber is cut and abandoned in the rush to get the largest trees out.

system giant corporations such as MacMillan Bloedel and British Columbia Forest Products are given twenty-five-year hegemonies over millions of acres of public forest. They can renew these licenses *ad infinitum*. In theory they are supposed to practice "integrated management" on these lands, to reforest, to protect the watersheds and to conserve enough habitat to ensure the survival of indigenous species. These requirements are seldom enforced.

On these tree farms it is not unusual for 25 percent of the marketable timber to be left lying on the ground after cutting, a practice that would make the worst U.S. "timber beast" blush. Environmental impact statements are unknown, and important salmon-producing drainages are destroyed without the slightest attempt at mitigation. Loggers often clear-cut right up to a bald eagle nesting site, leaving the single tree standing with no cover from the next big wind. Aside from all that, much of B.C.'s timber country has never been officially acquired from its Native American owners, who have subsisted on it for thousands of years. Recently native bands have begun court proceedings to reclaim forest land on Meares Island and in the Skeena River area, but the outcome is far from clear.

By U.S. standards, Canadian citizens have little influence on land-use decisions made by their provincial governments. Even a provincial park can be given over to logging and mining by administrative fiat, while conservationists have to be satisfied with seats on toothless advisory committees. Cameron Young, award-winning author of *The Forests of British Columbia,* estimates that at the current rate of 26 million cubic meters annually, that portion of B.C.'s coastal old growth that is now considered economic to log will have been liquidated in another seventeen years.

In spite of the large body of existing environmental law, U.S. conservationists have been scarcely more successful at protecting old growth on the Tongass or in the Northwest. Laws written to protect this mountain or that animal are not easily applied to an entire complex ecosystem, many of whose most important features are hidden from view. The scientific and long-term economic arguments for removing old growth forests from timber production fall largely outside the usual terms of conservationist dialectic, which thus far have been: Beauty, Bambi and Backpacking.

The first part of this *tripos* dates to John

The Stein Valley, tributary to the Fraser River northeast of Vancouver, is one of a very few—but magnificent—large tracts left unlogged in British Columbia. Native Indian bands are leading the fight to keep its trees from being pulped by mills in Boston Bar and Lytton.

Muir and reflects a public consensus he helped Theodore Roosevelt develop: that certain places ought to be beyond commercial reach for aesthetic or spiritual reasons alone. The second we owe to Aldo Leopold and other scientists of the 1930s, who preached the importance of habitat, helped forge the U.S. Fish and Wildlife Service and began a national system of wildlife refuges under Franklin Roosevelt. The third element reflects a growing interest in the outdoors and in the ecological health of the nation that reached the level of national consensus in the 1960s and 1970s, which was also the era of the Udalls and David Brower.

In each of these three epochs there existed a certain predisposition, a backlog of public understanding that allowed a consensus to form. Muir's and Teddy Roosevelt's constituents were the newly affluent urban middle class of the early 1900s. They owned the first practical automobiles and had the leisure to rediscover nature, which they viewed with late-romantic, almost religious, enthusiasm. Franklin Roosevelt, four decades later, freely admitted that he was responding to organized pressure from sportsmen, who clearly saw the waterfowl of a continent decimated by the droughts of the Dust Bowl years. And in the 1960s the Baby Boomers, the most affluent and best-educated bourgeoisie of them all, came of age, donned backpacks *en masse* and headed for the hills, where they discovered that the environment was in trouble.

Now the Baby Boomers have grown middle-aged and taken up golf. Slick timber company advertising portrays artificially maintained tree farms as the real thing, to a public which has never seen the real thing. The crisis in the old growth forest occurs at a time when environmentalism is on the back burner along with the space program. The relevant science is less

than twenty years old. When a handful of researchers began to suggest the wisdom of not cutting a great deal of valuable timberland to preserve "biotic diversity," few knew what they were talking about.

The timber industry itself has become sophisticated on the issue, of course, and is even becoming divided. In 1985 startled conservationists read this in the American Forestry Association's own journal:

> If the only reason for harvesting [old growth forests] is to keep afloat those timber industries and local economies that are on an inevitable crash-and-burn trajectory, then we say there is no reason to delay that inevitability with the sacrifice of never-to-be-replaced forest. . . . Let's not artificially prop up timber economies when all that would ultimately be accomplished is an irrevocably damaged heritage and an only

slightly delayed transition for communities that must look for other means of existence.

As of 1988 most Americans had never even heard of old growth. Still, one wonders how many Americans besides the members of Ducks Unlimited and the Audubon Society could have defined habitat in 1932. It is interesting to note that FDR allowed Aldo Leopold to create the national wildlife refuge system purely to get the duck hunters off his back. He never intended to fund it. He put the famous editorial cartoonist Ding Darling, who was a conservative Republican, in charge of the new U.S. Fish and Wildlife Service and gave him scarcely enough money for office supplies. Darling finally tricked the president by getting a rider attached to an omnibus bill that FDR signed, unread, just as he was leaving the White House for a fishing trip. It was weeks before anyone realized that Darling's

In the Central Cascades of Oregon, some of the oldest trees in the region have evolved along the waters of the Santiam River that flow out of Mt. Jefferson. This is a forest where frustrated environmentalists have blocked roads and sat in trees in attempts to stop the logging.

Like a detail of a chewed leaf, this aerial view of a portion of the Willamette and Mt. Hood National Forests near Mt. Hood shows the results of years of clear-cutting. More than one square mile of old growth forest is cut per week in Oregon and Washington.

rider was an appropriation of six million dollars for Leopold's refuges.

Darling's chicanery undoubtedly saved many species from extinction. Together with the Canadian lands bought or leased by a new private organization, Ducks Unlimited, the new refuges became the basis for what is by far the greatest international conservation success story in history.

In the case of old growth the time is as short as it was for waterfowl in the 1930s, the likely consequences for this continent much greater. Time and again, in China, in the Middle East and in North Africa, the destruction of vast forests has been followed by massive climatic change and the depletion of the soil. The former North African forest, for example, is now called the Sahara.

The best knowledge we possess suggests that a short-rotation managed forest on these soils will become increasingly expensive to maintain by the artificial means required as the nutrient levels drop. Furthermore, the danger of the herbicides and other chemicals necessary to maintain these artificial groves is becoming all too obvious. A public outcry in Oregon has led the forest service to cut back on helicopter sprays that have dioxin as one of their byproducts, but there is little control of the use of these relatives of Agent Orange on private lands. Apart from present risks, there is worldwide evidence that artificial forestry simply doesn't work. In parts of Europe three short rotations have been sufficient to thoroughly deplete the forest soil; while in much of China, it has taken only two.

It is entirely possible that we are creating a future "wet desert" in the Pacific Northwest. Nobody knows what that would do to annual rainfall levels in the region where more than half the hydroelectric power consumed in the United States is now generated. Jerry Frank-

60

lin suggests only half-jokingly that this new ecology might consist almost entirely of black-berry bushes. In that case spring runoffs might be so massive as to destroy our existing dam system. What other large-scale consequences we are bequeathing to our posterity is any-body's guess.

Nothing in human history prepares us for the sheer speed at which these unknown con-sequences are rushing toward us. In the last thirty years we have cut one-half of the world's forests at the rate of fifty acres per minute. More than 75 billion tons of topsoil have washed off previously forested lands in this century. Here in the U.S., land logged a century ago in Michigan still lies barren of trees, a cemetery of stumps. We've done this before. We know better.

The old growth forest of the Pacific North-west is by far the most productive of all the world's forests. Now, at the eleventh hour,

it has yielded up some of the most basic of its secrets. There is more to come. Before 1986, for example, no one guessed that the Pacific yew, a "trash tree" of the old growth under-story, was an important source of taxol, an anti-cancer drug. And it has become clear that, in the matter of learning to truly manage a forest for long-term productivity, we are kindergarteners.

That is a discovery that should surprise no one. Perhaps the most striking aspects of our depredation against the natural world in this century have been the confident arrogance with which we do it and the regularity with which we discover we were wrong. There's something depressingly moronic or retarded in that. Quantum mechanics has come up with the insight that "the universe is not only queerer than we suppose, but queerer than we *can* suppose." Biology has shown us, *via* Lewis Thomas, that organisms we took to be

This kind of second growth tree farm in the Oregon Coast Range is the real "biological desert," a term sometimes applied to old growth. When the young firs and hemlocks close ranks over a replanted clear-cut after about twenty years, the number of mammal species using it drops from twenty-five to about nine.

61

**Fog drifts through the canopy of old growth in the Oregon Coast Range.**

entities are in fact committees of other organisms. All the evidence suggests that nature consists of perfectly attuned linkages stretching out of our sight—and out of our understanding—in all directions. Yet we imagine we can destroy this forest and build another.

A single California red-backed vole, weighing about an ounce, his guts stuffed with mycorrhizal spores and nitrogen-producing bacteria, ventures out of cover to put those commodities precisely where they are needed. If the owl doesn't get him, he'll go back for more. It's his nature, programmed into his DNA over the millennia by natural selection. *He* is a forest manager. We cannot substitute ourselves for him. We can only watch him, and learn.

Sometime in the mid-1980s, and just for fun, some of the scientists at Oregon State University wrote a computer program to determine the cost of reproducing the functions of a single old growth Douglas fir tree by technological means. The total was very close to the cost of the U.S. space program from its inception to the time of Neal Armstrong's walk on the moon.

62

Redwoods—most massive forest in the world.

# THE WORLD'S CHAMPION FOREST

In the popular imagination, the densest forests are tropical jungles, the rain forests of the Congo or the Amazon basin. Taking into account all above-ground flora, stands of mature tropical rain forest have been recorded up to 415 metric tons per hectare (a metric ton equals 1.1 U.S. tons, a hectare is 2.47 acres).

But *average* above-ground biomass of old growth Douglas fir/western hemlock forest, the common type in western Oregon and Washington, is over twice that at 868 mt/ha. Total biomass in this type of forest has been recorded at up to 1590 mt/ha, *counting the stems alone*.

The greatest accumulation of plant mass ever recorded was a coast redwood stand in Humboldt State Park in California. Stem biomass alone was 3,461 mt/ha, and adding in branch, leaf and root biomass would increase the estimate of standing crop to well in excess of 4,000 mt/ha. The old growth can outproduce the jungle by a ratio of roughly seven to one!

Here are some maximal values for various forest types. Notice the high biomass that relatively young coastal Sitka spruce/western hemlock attains in the ultra-wet climate of the Alaskan panhandle and British Columbia.

| Type of Forest | Biomass (mt/ha) |
|---|---|
| coast redwood 1,000 yrs+ | 3,461 (stems only) |
| Douglas fir/western hemlock 250-1,000 yrs | 1,590 (stems only) |
| Sitka spruce/western hemlock 121-130 yrs | 1,163 (above ground) |
| temperate deciduous USA mature | 422 (includes shrubs, herbs) |
| tropical rain forest mature | 415 (includes shrubs, herbs) |

*Adapted from J. F. Franklin and R. H. Waring,
"Distinctive Features of the Northwestern Coniferous Forest"
in* Forests: Fresh Perspectives from Ecosystem Analysis.
*Corvallis: Oregon State University Press, 1979, pp. 60-61.*

63

Old growth forest,
Oregon.

**Spring growth of vine maple and elderberry arch over a small stream and the remains of an ancient big-leaf maple tree.**

Stream flows from the cedar forest on Long Island, Willapa Bay, Washington, which may have been undisturbed for 4,000 years.

Hemlock tree sprouts
from snag in old
growth.

Great Sitka spruce, the dominant tree near the Pacific coast.

Inner rotted wood spills from a stump overgrown with sword fern and twinflower vine.

Liverwort on rotting log.

An old stump in
southeast Alaska feeds
a garden of bunchberry.

Pink fawn lily.

Indian pipe and oxalis,
Washington.

Forest floor, Prince of
Wales Island, Alaska.

The life-giving embrace
of a young hemlock
around a long-dead
down tree.

Pacific rhododendron in
the old growth of the
Oregon Cascades.

The giant cedars of
Meares Island, B.C.,
rival the redwoods in
size but will be cut
unless local tribal
leaders, whose
ancestral lands these
are, win a pending court
case to keep control of
the island. (Photo
copyright Adrian Dorst)

# CHILDREN OF THE FOREST

It's midnight on a sixty-acre "hot burn" on the Andrews. The road down is temporarily engulfed by a firestorm fueled by an enormous slash pile, so I am lying on my back watching the hunt of an opportunistic nighthawk. Very likely *Chordeiles minor* is dining on arthropods he's never seen before tonight. The heat column is terrific and all sorts of insects are being borne up.

Fire Boss Charlie Bodie has every technician on the Blue River Ranger District up here tonight with enough hoses and canvas reservoirs and gasoline-powered pumps to guard a sizable town. Deliberate burns are usually much slower and cooler, but the purpose tonight is to simulate a disastrous wildfire. Biologist Phil Sollins—distinguishable from the rest of the yellow-jacketed, hard-hatted crew by the long loaf of French bread sticking out of his rucksack—will inherit the charred remains. He will plant these acres with test plots of *Ceanothus*—snowbrush—long considered an obnoxious weed by forest managers, something to be zapped from a helicopter with defoliants like Agent Orange because it competes for light and scarce nutrients with young Douglas fir seedlings.

But it seems possible that early successional plants like this one form a part of the forest's

**Slash burning, here silhouetting a remnant stand of trees in Oregon, is commonly used to clear the way for replanting after a clear-cut. Such burning robs the next forest of valuable small animal habitat and the slow release of nutrients.**

fail-safe mechanism we haven't understood, perhaps a means of fixing nitrogen, enriching the soil, or deflecting the attention of deer—those age-old experts at brush control and pre-commercial thinning. Deer have evolved to fear wolves, Aldo Leopold once noted; so why should we not also suppose that mountains have evolved to fear deer? Sollins will attempt to read another page of the forest's book.

Meanwhile some exciting news crackles over the walkie-talkies of the fire crews: a mountain lion has been sighted prowling the edge of the burn for small mammals driven out by the flames. We are pleased by this glimpse, perhaps because we, too, are hunter-gatherers, bipedal fellow predators.

Driving over the high ridges earlier this September evening I had time to notice the human tribe at work: beekeepers had moved their trailers up into the subalpine meadows to live by their hives for the gathering of salal and

fireweed honey. Bow hunters were hiking in to crouch along the game trails and the rifle season was not far off. A man and his son field-dressed grouse by the side of the road, anxious no doubt to get the carcasses exposed to the breeze as soon as possible. Another man from the town had brought his wife and children to gather huckleberries in the reddening clear-cuts while he wandered off for a bit of game scouting. There was competition for the berries though: when I stopped to get a few for my own children I noticed bear scat everywhere.

And, of course, there were the large-scale gatherers, the teams of tree fallers oiling their chain saws alongside battered pickup trucks at the end of another dangerous day's work.

Perhaps it would be good for the forest if we were more honest with ourselves about our status as hunter-gatherers. More than 42 million people in America hunt or fish, accord-

ing to a U.S. Fish and Wildlife Service report, a vast if disorganized constituency with a direct stake in the continued existence of old growth. Repeatedly in the last decade they have been fed a line of familiar old malarkey. "Hell, if we cut the old growth the owl would supposedly vanish and if we don't cut it the elk will vanish," complained John Crowell to reporters at the 1982 North American Wildlife Conference. Even then it was apparent that ignorance was bliss at the political appointee level of government. Downstairs at the same conference some of the Reagan administration's professional-level employees were reporting a strong positive link between Roosevelt elk populations and old growth. The study, a cooperative effort of the BLM and the Oregon Department of Fish and Wildlife, suggested that elk seek the cover of big trees in summer as well as winter to regulate their body temperatures and to digest food more efficiently.

Alaska State Fish and Game Department biologist John Schoen reported even more striking discoveries about the Tongass National Forest's 40 thousand Sitka blacktailed deer. By using radio telemetry he was able to confirm that Sitkas avoid second growth as scrupulously as do spotted owls. Furthermore, they make use of every portion of the old growth according to a precise pattern dictated by heat, cold, rain and snow. They could easily be wiped out by logging, along with the region's otters and the world-famous "brown" bears, largest of all the grizzlies. Schoen's findings have the Alaska Department of Fish and Game locked in a struggle with the Forest Service over the few intact watersheds left in the Tongass.

But the destruction of prime elk and deer habitat is a mere peccadillo compared with what has happened to the fisheries of the for-

Roosevelt elk, like Sitka blacktailed deer, are dependent on old growth for summer cooling and for forage when deep snows cover open areas. Studies show that when too much forest is cut, elk populations decline by as much as one-half. (Photo copyright Tom and Pat Leeson)

In a pioneering study lead by James Sedell of Oregon State University, researchers snorkel in an old growth stream to count fish and aquatic animals. Results confirm a great loss in diversity after logging.

Salmon moving toward
spawning grounds rely
on the temperature and
sediment control
exercised by old growth
on streams whose flow
is regulated by logs and
woody debris.

ested Northwest. Combing old cannery records, James Sedell, another of Jerry Franklin's co-authors, estimated that between 1889 and 1896 a single small Oregon coastal river, the Siuslaw, had an average annual run of about 218,750 coho salmon. The Siuslaw is one of thirty major rivers and streams along the Oregon coast. The total management goal for all thirty these days is less than 250,000 fish. It isn't being met.

Accounts written in the nineteenth century about Northwest rivers describe them as choked with woody debris along their entire lengths, not just in steep coastal terrain but in the broad inland valleys as well. In 1870 the Willamette River flowed in five separate channels along much of its length. Sediment pools, marshes and sloughs abounded. The old growth forest gave these rivers the same essential characteristics found only in small headwater streams today.

But by 1900 a huge "improvement" program had begun. Unless they had already been channeled to create farmland, the rivers were de-snagged, blasted and scoured for log drives or the passage of commerce. By the time fisheries scientists noticed steep declines in spawning populations in the 1920s, the original nature of Northwest rivers had been forgotten.

Now Sedell is studying the streamside and underwater habitat of old growth forest streams to confirm and explain his historical insight. For example, a census of several small headwater streams in the Cascades noted that in a clear-cut area species diversity dropped to one: rainbow trout less than one year old.

Pools and backwaters tend to disappear in heavily logged areas, and surveys of coastal streams in Oregon have revealed that populations of salmon are directly related to available pool volume. In addition, such species as

"The renewable resource?" This once lush portion of the Oregon Coast Range reflects our stewardship: everywhere in the Northwest forests have been cleared permanently for settlement, only partially replanted, or allowed to grow back only to be cut again after a relatively short time. For whatever reasons, old growth is gone from 90 percent of its range.

coho salmon, steelhead and older cutthroat trout require the protective cover of large woody debris, particularly in steep mountain rivers. The Siuslaw, mentioned above, was once so choked with logs that early explorers couldn't get up it.

Sedell's findings suggest a management direction for Oregon and Washington, though stream restoration is likely to be a long and expensive process in these states. But the news comes in time to help save some of the still pristine rivers of the Alaskan panhandle, potentially the greatest sport and commercial salmon fishery left on earth.

The principle management controversy, though, centers on large trees. For a half-century before intensive logging began to deface the Tongass, for example, the panhandle forests were selectively cut for the tall, straight Sitka spruce needed for masts and derricks. There was no lasting damage to the ecosystem from this activity. And there need be no lasting impairment of Douglas fir forests from the extraction of a controlled amount of clear vertical grain lumber. Ordinary construction no longer requires sawn structural timber even for wood buildings, since glue-laminates and particle board products, which lend themselves to automated production, can do the jobs as well or better. A pathetic foot-

note to the old growth tragedy is that much of this forest is being permanently erased from the face of the earth to make twenty or thirty years' worth of ordinary plywood that could just as easily come out of second growth.

In 1985 a young activist named Cecelia Ostrow circulated a letter to people interested in protecting old growth. Ostrow's letter cited the frustration she and others had encountered in trying to make a case for this forest in the absence of figures showing how much of it actually existed. Instead she suggested a flat ban on further cutting of any Douglas fir that was 250 years old or older, more than three feet in diameter at chest height, and met the other criteria listed by Franklin *et al* in *Characteristics of Old Growth Douglas Fir Forests*. Ostrow went on to say that similar criteria should be spelled out for the other principle species, and that the ban should extend to non-old growth acres needed to protect old growth from the kind of degradation that had occurred in California's Redwood National Park where clear-cutting extended right up to the park borders.

Ostrow's "radical" solution struck a chord with many more moderate conservationists who were faced with the same statistical problem. In fact, change the open-ended word *ban* to the more limited term *moratorium*, and Ostrow's proposal was identical to what government scientists had been saying among themselves—but not publicly, for fear of their jobs. As soon as Chris Maser had resigned from the BLM, for example, he began to advocate a two-year moratorium on logging in old growth, long enough for a real inventory to be done. Jerry Franklin, still a half-time U.S. Forest Service employee, will not say he favors such a step but adds, "with the right kind of funding I could get the inventory done in *one* year."

Ever since the post-WWII housing boom, district and regional foresters have been under pressure to exaggerate the timber base—the total acreage of commercially valuable trees in their jurisdictions—in order to end up with the largest possible "allowable cut"—the percentage of the base that can be removed in

PARDON ME
THOU BLEEDING PIECE
OF EARTH
THAT I AM MEEK
AND GENTLE WITH THESE
BUTCHERS.

*Shakespeare*

(Poster courtesy
Husband-Pothier)

The boundary between private forest land (left) and an uncut area of Willamette National Forest in Oregon. Heavy logging of industry-owned land has increased the pressure on the Forest Service and Bureau of Land Management to dedicate more and more public acreage to the saw.

any given year. Thus figures that reflect the real world are practically non-existent. For example, in January 1988, Al Burkardt, Director of Timber Management Planning for Region Six, said there were 5,400,000 acres of old growth available for cutting on the region, which covers all of Washington, most of Oregon and a little of northern California.

On the other hand estimates from several government scientists who have studied the matter over the last decade averaged about 2.7 million acres. Jerry Franklin thinks the number is somewhere between 2 million and 2.5 million.

Figures on how much large, low-elevation old growth is "safe" inside national parks and wilderness areas are equally hard to come by. Industry spokesmen say millions of acres, some conservationists say at most a few hundred thousand.

No sensible public debate about the future of this forest can take place until such a massive uncertainty is resolved.

U.S. Senator Mark Hatfield, the ranking Republican member of the Senate Appropriations Committee, made it clear in 1987 that there would be no more wilderness created out of commercial timberlands while he sat on the committee. Hatfield's statement adequately expresses the view held by such corporate leaders as Willamette Industries' Swindells, who predict economic disaster for the Northwest in the event of a moratorium.

Experts outside both the industry and the conservation organizations take a different view. For example, Douglas Brodie, a forest economist at Oregon State University, thinks that the effect of a two-year moratorium would be minimal since, with a four-year backlog of sales to offer, the Forest Service could simply shift the same resources over to non-old growth.

If Franklin's estimate turns out to be correct, we may well be where Ostrow and those who agree with her think we are: at the moment where only a perpetual ban can save this ecosystem. Even that might not mean that all logging in old growth would cease. Franklin points out that small (less than three hundred acres) freestanding groves can be impossible to manage, if for no other reason than that deer and elk tend to "yard up" in them and destroy the understory. Most scientists we spoke to expressed a preference for whole watersheds, or stands otherwise protected, for example, by borders with other protected lands.

The most coherent vision of a future for the old growth to date is the work of Larry D. Harris, professor in the Department of Wildlife and Range Sciences, School of Forest Resources and Conservation, at the University of Florida. In *The Fragmented Forest* (University of Chicago Press, 1984), Harris argues for a series of old growth islands, an archipelago linked by corridors to extend the effective range of species threatened by confinement. The islands in Harris's old growth archipelago would vary in size: the smaller ones would have better corridors of communication with adjacent islands to make up for their lack of size, and would also be buffered from adjacent development by surrounding belts of forest on long-rotation management. Larger islands would require less protection and some species would live out their entire life cycles within them.

Harris is a proponent of Island Biogeographic Theory, a discipline that takes into account not merely the numbers of a species needed for survival and the range requirements of a given population, but also genetic diversity within a species, the biotic diversity needed for health. It recognizes that not all old

**Every acre of the mature old growth forest is slightly different, reacting to a slightly different set of influences. It would seem prudent to view each portion of the forest as an individual landscape when decisions are made for logging or preservation.**

87

Old growth: a 7-foot wide Douglas fir, open forest floor, well-spaced trees with clear stems rising 100 feet to the first branch. These trees have been growing undisturbed for over 500 years.

growth stands are equal in their ability to support such health. It recognizes that some species might survive best on one or a few large preserves, while others, the farthest-ranging and hence most threatened, are best served by many well-linked smaller stands. Best of all, Harris's archipelago concept offers forest managers some flexibility, taking into account the inevitability of development. Harris writes:

> In the human-dominated landscape of the future, many species will not have a "continental" source pool of potential colonizers other than those maintained within the system of preserves . . . (for example, North American grizzly bears or large herbivores in African parks). This means that the degree to which the habitat island system functions in a multiple-use environment will determine survival or extinction for a con-

siderable number of species. Based on the combined body of wildlife biology information and general ecological principles, I believe that an island system chosen by design will be superior to one inherited by default.

Harris argues strongly for the preservation of existing old growth until such an archepelago can be designed. His scheme also requires timber managers to plan for substantial amounts of timber in the 120- to 200-year age class, called "mature" in industry jargon (old growth is "overmature"). The biological value of a small stand of old growth is greatly increased if adjacent to mature timber that shares some of its characteristics. The destructive pressure of deer and elk mentioned by Franklin, for example, can be greatly lessened.

There is almost no mature timber in the present forest inventory, and managing for

very much of it is sure to cause an outcry. Industry is used to cutting managed forests at 120, 80, or even 60 years. Implementing the archipelago idea in Canada, though, will be even tougher: an estimated 99 percent of commercial timber there is old growth.

Harris's archepelago concept is a masterstroke, for it offers us a way to salvage all or most of the features of an ecosystem that now lies about us in shreds and tatters, to "keep every cog and wheel," as Aldo Leopold warned us to do. An old growth moratorium is the first step, and that would reduce the amount of timber coming off federal forests in the Northwest by about 50 percent. Industry spokesmen are forever saying they need that timber until their own second growth "comes on line." They have been saying that for four decades. They cite the jobs that will be lost. Meanwhile they themselves have been eliminating jobs as fast as they can. Between 1979 and 1985, for

example, 15,400 jobs were eliminated in plywood mills and sawmills in Oregon.

A decade ago, mills that produced two thousand board feet of veneer for plywood per employee/shift were considered efficient. At the beginning of the 1980s mills began coming on line that could better that by one third. Now mills have been developed that can turn out more than ten thousand board feet per employee/shift, utilizing trees up to forty inches in diameter. Such a mill requires two truckloads of logs each day just to keep one employee on the payroll.

Mitigating the effect of jobs lost due to a political decision to stop cutting old growth is not beyond our means if one considers the cost of road building in these same forests. George T. Frampton, Jr., president of the Wilderness Society, wrote in the Summer 1987 issue of *Wilderness* that in 1985, a good year for timber sales, the Forest Service spent $600 million more for road building and administrative costs than it took in in timber receipts. User fees and other income made up some of this deficit; overall the agency lost only 400 million taxpayer dollars! The Forest Service now maintains 343,000 miles of its own roads, more than eight times the length of the entire interstate highway system. It has plans to build 580,000 more miles at a cost of $200 million per year.

Stopping, or at least slowing down, this bureaucratic juggernaut would be one side effect of Ostrow's and the scientists' proposals. The savings could make up for every dime of lost income in the affected states several times over.

Those individual national forests that do make a profit do so, ironically, from the sale of high-volume old growth. They would have to turn their attention elsewhere. Fortunately, there is plenty to do. In 1984, for example, the Forest Service met 98 percent of its timber cutting goals, and 140 percent of its road building goals, a whopping excess. But it met only 24 percent of its trail construction goals, 34 percent of its wildlife habitat improvement goals and 28 percent of its soil and water improvement goals.

A moratorium on logging old growth must be instituted without delay, and an inventory begun. The decision of how much old growth to save may be, as Jerry Franklin suggests, a social and a moral question; but there is no escaping the fact that it is a scientific and an economic one as well. The public, whose forest this is, deserves to know *what* it is, and what it is likely to be worth as an investment in the nation's future. The bottom line is likely to be a lot more than thirty years' worth of plywood sold to a shrinking number of entrepreneurs at a dead loss.

Meanwhile, up here on the firelit Andrews, a lion still prowls the edges of a forest that is half a millennium old. Chris Maser has tales to tell about mountain lions that have stalked him. Once he wrote:

> During the first snow flurries of winter, one of these cats stayed more or less abreast of me for the better part of three days. I never saw the cat but I easily found its tracks by backtracking or by circling. Even though at times I could "feel" its presence, its stealth was remarkable. I sensed a distinct feeling of companionship with this silent traveller and felt sad when the cat departed.

These could easily be the last days of America's last great forest. Chris Maser and Larry Harris point out that one third of the 118 vertebrate species that find primary habitat there find it nowhere else. Time has all but run out for the spotted owl, the marbled murrelet, the pileated woodpecker, the fisher, the marten, the cougar. It seems a tall order to recapture, at the eleventh hour, a sense of kinship with Maser's great cat and all he represents, to relearn the truth that "this is our habitat. This is the habitat of the human race."

But the ticking clock is *our* problem, not the forest's. "Look," Maser says, "we've imposed time restraints on a system that knows none and doesn't recognize them. Seen from a distance, we must look like a bivouac of army ants. We're specialists who practice the art of extinction."

Mill with second growth harvest.

First bridge across the South Fork Brietenbush River in Oregon, built after citizen appeals to stay the logging of this virgin area were denied by the Forest Service. A court has since required reconsideration of the appeals.

Even a small stand of ancient trees, like this grove saved in an Oregon county park, reminds us of the power and spirit in the old growth.

In autumn, when other hunters mark their stands on the ridge lines and the edges of high clear-cuts, I push through the tangled alder along old growth stream bottoms, looking for signs of a crossing place. It is the wisdom in my family that here is where the bucks will come when they are afraid. When I have found the place, I will come back to it before dawn and hide myself a few yards off with the wind at my face. In time, no doubt, the deer will learn, or evolve, to fear such places; but for now, I need only sit still.

Doing nothing comes hard to Americans. Our feet want to walk on over the next ridge; our palms itch for the haft of a tool. We seek enterprises; we held the Native American in contempt because he appeared to want and do so little. Yet he would take one slab from a cedar for his lodge, and the tree lived; he took a few fish from one part of the stream, and moved camp; he took a deer from one herd, and then left that herd alone for a while. The tree, the fish, the deer were usually there, close by, when he needed them again.

Sit still long enough, I've learned, and the forest goes about its business. One, two otters come out to play in the stream. A woodpecker, silent since I came, starts up its jackhammer work again. A hundred rustlings in the nearby leaves and mosses signal the presence of voles and mice. A caddis hatch swarms in a shaft of sunlight. A shifting wisp of wind brings me the tang of animal decay. Something falls from the canopy. Something big goes thump not far off and my hackles rise: maybe it's a bear!

Once in a Canadian forest I got to watch a bull moose as big as a house foraging. He ate a few leaves from a bush, moved on, ate a few from another bush, moved on again. He didn't damage any one bush enough to kill it — which struck me as good policy.

Do nothing for as long as it takes, and what you should do, often as not, comes clear into a mind not clouded by activity. It's called meditation, or putting yourself in the middle of things.

Sitting by the stream downwind of a deer crossing, I am in the middle of the old growth, its myriad linkages stretching out away from me in time and space, its billions of niches filled with purposes I can only guess. Some don't like to call this the work of God; but it sure isn't the work of man. Maybe the forest will give me a venison for the Thanksgiving table today, and maybe it won't. At the end of a day in these woods, I find I've always gotten what I came for.

It seems incredible to think it, here under the high canopy, but as a society we've got this forest surrounded now. We've cut it down to size at last. The Hindus of India, who have a myth for any occasion, have a myth for this, too. An evil dragon drinks up the River of Life. All its waters are contained within his swollen belly. In order for life to go on, he must be slain. Indra slits the dragon open with his sword, killing it. The waters gush forth, and the world is reborn.

We have nearly swallowed up this continent's last great forest, and unlike some nations in the tropics who are doing the same thing (as we have taught them), we can't use poverty as an excuse.

We are edge-dwelling children of this forest. We cannot tell if we evolved for it or it for us. It would seem prudent to leave some of it, as well as other parts of our habitat, alone. For we have seen how men live and die in the depleted lands of the earth. There is no reason to suppose our suicidal greed will end in anything as kind as a stroke from Indra's sword.

**Timber sale protest, South Brietenbush River, Oregon.**

APPENDIX A

# ONE FOREST, MANY BATTLEGROUNDS

In a struggle that involves twenty U.S. National Forests, Bureau of Land Management holdings and all of western British Columbia and some private lands, conservationists, Native Americans and scientists contend with industry and forest bureaucrats for this continent's "last big woods."

*Alaska:* Efforts continue to get legislation through Congress that would cancel fifty-year timber contracts and force planners on the Tongass to face budget scrutiny each year. The Southeast Alaska Conservation Council also wants designation of deserving wilderness areas to protect key habitat areas and the panhandle's economically important fishery.

Among the most important old growth areas are:

• Lands adjacent to Upper Hoona Sound and Tenakee Inlet on Chicagof Island, where many rivers such as the Kadashan and Lisianski curve through stands of giant spruce, hemlock and cedar to form lush meadowlands and some of the most productive tidal flats on earth. Their enormous animal and bird populations are threatened by logging within the next five years.

• The southern portion of Kuiu Island, where intricate, salmon-rich inlets like Bay of Pillars, Affleck Canal and No Name Bay support commercial and subsistence fishing which will be severely damaged if planned cutting by Alaska Pulp Company fills the waterways with logs.

• Noyes, Baker, Lulu and San Fernando islands, small outliers of clear-cut-ravaged Prince of Wales Island. These are important centers of fishing and subsistence hunting.

• Yakutat Forelands, 200,000 acres in the far north of the Tongass is home of a truly "virgin" forest—one still evolving 500-800 years after the retreat of glaciers from the St. Elias Range. Although not classic old growth, these trees are rare and important ecologically, yet would be clear-cut under present Forest Service ten-year plans.

*British Columbia:* "Super Natural B.C.," the tourism ads call it. Tourists of the near future may indeed have to be in tune with the spirit world to enjoy nature here. Some estimates give the remaining old growth of the coast and the Fraser Valley less than twenty years to live. Some nine million acres of cutover land lie inadequately reforested.

Conservation groups have had little influence on the provincial government, which controls most of the timberlands and has traditionally sided with the big logging companies. But Native Americans have begun to find political clout. The Haida succeeded in drawing international attention to threatened forests and estuaries on South Moresby Island in the Queen Charlottes. A national park was established there in 1987. Further south, just off the west coast of Vancouver Island, native bands have gone to court to protect the groves of Meares Island from the chain saws of Mac-Millan Bloedel.

Few other large tracts of old growth remain in British Columbia. Among the most important:

- Megin River, Vancouver Island. This magnificent watershed would make a logical addition to Strathcona Provincial Park. But park status doesn't necessarily mean protection in Canada: activists were recently jailed during protests against a government decision to allow mining within Strathcona's boundaries.
- Tsitika River Valley, one of the last remaining uncut areas on northern Vancouver Island. The river flows into Robson Bight, a pristine estuary known worldwide as a haven for orca whales.
- Khutzeymateen Inlet and river, north of Prince Rupert. A 143-square-mile watershed that remains pristine largely because of its remote location, this area boasts an immense annual salmon run and a thriving population of giant coast grizzlies. Nevertheless, timber planners have targeted its stands of giant Sitka spruce. Conservationists claim that logging the trees would mean a net loss to the public of some $10 million.
- The Stein River, which flows into the Fraser northeast of Vancouver through a narrow valley that has been home to the Lytton and Mt. Currie Indian bands for centuries. The natives are leading the fight to keep British Columbia Forest Products from punching roads across their sacred ground, abounding with pictographs and active cultural sites, to get a few choice old growth stands deep within the valley.

*Washington:* A signal victory for old growth proponents was the inclusion of seven thousand acres in the Clearwater Wilderness established just north of Mt. Rainier National Park in 1984. A major old growth wilderness at Boulder Creek was established at the same time. Since then some sales, notably on the Gifford Pinchot National Forest, have been temporarily halted; but most of the state's old growth is still in the commercial timber base.

After heavy lobbying by old growth advocates, Washington's state government is taking an interest in the protection of old growth, one not seen in neighboring Oregon. The Washington State Wildlife Commission has officially listed the northern spotted owl as endangered, something the federal government has so far been unwilling to do. The State Department of Natural Resources controls a significant amount of old growth and has halted or slowed down timber sales in some owl habitat areas.

An unusual remnant forest of giant cedar trees, thought by Jerry Franklin to have been undisturbed by major fire or storm for 4,000 years, has been purchased, after lengthy negotiations, from Weyerhaeuser Corporation and is now under the protection of the U.S. Fish and Wildlife Service in Willapa National Wildlife Refuge. Weyerhaeuser, however, may log off all the surrounding forest. A buffer area would be highly desirable if this unique stand is to be preserved.

Other critical areas in Washington include:

- Damfino Creek, 5,800 acres of old growth along the Canadian border known for its marten, pileated woodpeckers, cougars and bears. Though adjacent to Mt. Baker Wilderness Area, it was excluded from past wilderness legislation after heavy lobbying by timber interests. It is scheduled to be sold in 1990.
- White Chuck Roadless Area. A popular recreation area featuring a hot spring and easy access to the oft-climbed southern flank of Glacier Peak, the White Chuck would have long been included in either the Glacier Peak Wilderness or the North Cascades National Park were it not for relentless pressure from timber interests.
- Pratt River, a rarity in heavily logged western Washington: an old growth wilderness just an hour from downtown Seattle. Here nature has intervened on her own behalf as the Middle Fork of the Snowqualmie River has repeatedly washed out attempts to drive logging roads into the valley. The lower

slopes were partially logged during the railroad days of the 1930s, but many pristine acres remain—for now.

- Dark Divide, 58,000 acres of the Gifford Pinchot National Forest which constitute the largest de facto wilderness in southern Washington. In addition to old growth, the Divide contains ridge tops and flowered meadows with unequaled views of Mts. Ranier, Adams and St. Helens. But it has shrunk by half since 1960, and those areas not slated for future logging are being degraded by increased off-road vehicle access.

- 13-Mile Basin, across the Cascades in the Kettle Range, Colville National Forest. This superb remnant of old growth ponderosa pine has been saved only through decade-long litigation and administrative appeal by local conservationists. The basin's streams, rich in salmon, flow through the adjacent Colville Indian Reservation and are an important subsistence resource.

*Oregon:* 1987 was an especially black year in Oregon as an eight-hundred-year-old stand on the Middle Santiam River (Willamette National Forest) was chain-sawed while negotiations still continued in court. In the Mowhawk Valley local citizens were accustomed to using one 110-acre old growth stand as a park. But the Bureau of Land Management decided otherwise: a third was cut, another third sold for cutting. Especially sharp conflicts are being fought in Oregon over stands such as:

- Larch Mountain area, one of the glories of the Columbia Gorge National Scenic Area. Mt. Hood National Forest's draft management plans suggest including in the timber-selling base as much of its 2,000 old growth acres as possible before permanent regulations replace interim guidelines in the brand-new scenic area. Possible future timber sales include the headwater groves of several of the gorge's most spectacular waterfalls, including world-renowned Multnomah Falls.

- The ponderosa pine areas, located in central Oregon on the east side of the Cascades.

These are scattered stands of the ancient "yellow bellies," as the pines are locally called. Supporters ranging from the president of an electronics corporation to local ranchers are involved in the effort to save areas like Squaw Creek, where canyon rims protect old growth pines right down to the edge of the wild Deschutes River.

- Santiam River, a forest complex on the west side of the Cascades. Though heavily logged, it still contains some of the state's finest unprotected stands along Pyramid Creek and the Three Creeks area, where the "preemptive strike" at the so-called Millennium Grove took place. Perhaps chief among these is the 10,000-acre stand on Opal Creek, which contains some of the largest Douglas firs and cedars in the state.

- The Siskiyous, Oregon's ancient coastal range, including the Kalmiopsis, where grow strange plants found nowhere else on earth. Currently old growth defenders are trying to keep Siskiyou National Forest from salvage logging areas of big trees that endured, and were not destroyed by, great fires in 1987—mute evidence that old growth withstands fire much better than adjacent tree farms.

*California:* The paltry 4 percent that is left of the redwoods—the tallest trees on earth—is concentrated in roadside state parks, Redwoods National Park, which was seriously damaged by logging right up to its boundaries, and in a few remaining private forests. Any hope of saving this ecosystem thus hinges on the good will of private landholders, and the state itself has no inventory of, nor policy to protect, these holdings.

What that can mean was made clear recently when the Maxxam Group, a holding company, engineered a takeover of the Pacific Lumber Company, which had been practicing selective logging on its Humboldt County lands for decades, and planned to do so indefinitely.

Perhaps the executives of Maxxam knew little about timber management, or if they knew, that weighed less in the balance than the $795 million debt they'd incurred to buy Pacific. According to the *New York Times,* in order to liquidate that debt they decided to clear-cut much of Pacific's old growth timber, a move insiders predicted would soon put the company out of business and its employees out of their jobs. Caught in the financial cross fire and apparently doomed: the Headwaters Wilderness, an 8,000-acre grove of irreplaceable redwoods.

And so the fight continues, with increasing desperation as the ecosystem is more and more degraded. This book is limited in its scope to the Pacific Northwest; but it must not be forgotten that hard fights are going on to preserve old growth forests elsewhere: the giant Sequoia in south-central California, and lodgepole pine, Douglas fir, western larch and ponderosa pine forests in the intermountain region and the Rockies.

APPENDIX B

# ORGANIZATIONS CONCERNED WITH OLD GROWTH

Audubon Society – National Forest Issues
801 Pennsylvania Ave., SE
Washington, DC 20003
(202) 547-9009

Audubon Society
PO Box 462
Olympia, WA 98507
(206) 786-8020

Breitenbush Community
Breitenbush Box 578
Detroit, OR 97342
(503) 854-3501

Earth First!
P.O. Box 5871
Tucson, AZ 85703
(602) 622-1371

National Wildlife Federation
519 SW 3rd Ave.
Portland, OR 97204
(503) 222-1429

North Coast Environmental Center
712 8th Ave.
Trinidad, CA 95570
(707) 822-6918

Oregon Natural Resources Council
1161 Lincoln St.
Eugene, OR 97401
(503) 344-0675

Sierra Club – Northwest
1516 Melrose
Seattle, WA 98122
(206) 621-1696

Sierra Club – National Forest Issues
330 Pennsylvania Ave., SE
Washington, DC 20003
(202) 547-1144

Southeast Alaska Conservation Council
PO Box 21692
Juneau, AK 99802
(907) 586-6942

Western Canada Wilderness Committee
1520 West 6th
Vancouver, BC, V6J 1R2, CANADA
(604) 731-6716

The Wilderness Society
1424 4th St., Suite 822
Seattle, WA 98101
(206) 624-6430

The Wilderness Society – National
Forest Issues
1400 I St., NW
Washington, DC 20005
(202) 828-6600

# Selected Bibliography

## Books:

Arno, Stephen, and Hammerly, Ramona. *Northwest Trees*. Seattle: The Mountaineers, 1977.

Franklin, Jerry, and Dryness, C. T. *Natural Vegetation of Oregon and Washington*. Portland, OR: U.S. Department of Agriculture Pacific Northwest Forest and Range Experiment Station, 1973.

Franklin, Jerry, et al. *Ecological Characteristics of Old Growth Douglas Fir Forests*. Portland, OR: U.S. Department of Agriculture Pacific Northwest Forest and Range Experiment Station, 1981.

Harris, Larry D. *The Fragmented Forest*. Chicago: University of Chicago Press, 1984.

Islands Protection Society. *Islands at the Edge*. Vancouver, B.C.: Douglas and McIntyre, 1984.

Ketchum, Glenn, and Ketchum, Carey. *The Tongass, Alaska's Vanishing Rainforest*. New York: Aperture, 1987.

Leopold, Aldo. *Sand County Almanac and Essays from the Round River*. New York: Ballantine/Oxford University Press, 1966.

Maser, Chris. *The Redesigned Forest*. San Pedro, CA: R. and E. Miles, 1988.

Maser, Chris, and Mate, Bruce. *Natural History of Oregon Coast Mammals*. Portland, OR: U.S. Department of Agriculture Pacific Northwest Forest and Range Experiment Station, 1981.

Maser, Chris, and Trappe, James. *The Seen and Unseen World of the Fallen Tree*. Portland, OR: U.S. Department of Agriculture Pacific Northwest Forest and Range Experiment Station, 1984.

Myers, Norman. *The Primary Source*. New York: W. W. Norton, 1984. Deals with world forest problems.

Pyle, Robert Michael. *Wintergreen*. New York: Charles Scribner's Sons, 1986.

Schrepfer, Susan. *The Fight to Save the Redwoods*. Madison: University of Wisconsin Press, 1983.

Spurr, S. H., and Barnes, Burton. *Forest Ecology, Third Edition*. New York: John Wiley and Sons, Inc., 1980.

Wallace, David Rains. *The Klamath Knot*. San Francisco: Sierra Club Books, 1983.

Whitney, Stephen. *The Audubon Society Nature Guides: Western Forests*. New York: Alfred A. Knopf, 1985.

Young, Cameron, et al. *Forests of British Columbia*. Vancouver: Whitecap, 1985.

## Articles:

Baker, Dean. "Virgin Forests Under Fire." *National Wildlife*, February-March 1986.

Carey, John. "The Roads Less Traveled." *National Wildlife*, April-May 1988.

Daniel, John. "The Long Dance of the Trees." *Wilderness*. Spring 1988.

Kelly, David, and Braasch, Gary. "The Decadent Forest." *Audubon*, March 1986.

Laycock, George. "Trashing the Tongass." *Audubon*, November 1987.

McKee, Russell, and Sams, Carl R. "Tombstones of a Lost Forest." *Audubon*, March 1988.

M'Gonigle, Michael, and Alden, Ted. "Wilderness Epitaph." *Equinox*. September/October 1986. Details British Columbia forest destruction.

"Of Trees and Hope in the National Forests." *Wilderness*, Summer 1983. A special issue.

Wilcove, David S. "What I Saw When I Went to the Forest." *Wilderness*. Spring 1988.